THIS BOOK BELONGS TO:

**Praise for Allen Klein,
the world's only Jollytologist®, and his books**

"I am always looking for ideas that help people enrich their lives. *The Art of Living Joyfully* does just that. I highly recommend you read it and embrace its wise, and sometimes witty, words. They will feed your soul, lift your spirits, and help you live a fuller, richer, and more joy-filled life."

—SARK (Susan Ariel Rainbow Kennedy),
author of *Living Juicy*

"I have come to know that sometimes the simplest words can make a major difference in how people perceive and interact with their world. This book can make that same difference to you."

—Jack Canfield,
coauthor of the *Chicken Soup for the Soul* series

"Allen Klein is a noble and vital force watching over the human condition."

—Jerry Lewis

"Allen Klein has a way of authentically bringing the gift of humor to every aspect of life. *The Art of Living Joyfully* reminds you to choose laughter as your companion every day. Don't just buy this book—live it!"

—Terry Paulson, PhD,
author of *The Optimism Advantage*

"Allen Klein has done it again in *The Art of Living Joyfully*! He gives us common sense advice that nourishes joy in all areas of our life. If you are hungry for more joy in your life, then this is a must-have book."

—Susyn Reeve, author of *The Inspired Life*

"Regardless of the situations that life throws at us, Allen teaches us to laugh loudly, love passionately, and live our lives joyfully. Let Allen inspire you to embrace and celebrate the joy in your life and in the life that surrounds you."

—Carole Brody Fleet,
author of *Happily Even After*

"Take these words and love them—take these words and LIVE them!"

—BJ Gallagher,
author of *It's Never Too Late to Be What You Might Have Been*

"The world's only Jollytologist® is the one I turn to when I need jollying. Allen Klein got into the business of joy when he learned the healing power of humor; he has been on the case ever since. *The Art of Living Joyfully* will take up permanent residence on my desk and within easy reach so I can get morning reminders of how to be happy EVERY DAY!"

—Nina Lesowitz,
coauthor of *Living Life as a Thank You*

"This powerful collection of quotes serves as a great reminder of simple truths and timeless wisdom that can alter our lives in a profound way. This book is guaranteed to inspire all who read it!"

—Mike Robbins,
author of *Focus on the Good Stuff*

"I use quotations in all my books and presentations. A funny, profound, inspiring quote is a quick way to spice up material. Allen's collection is a great place to find some never-before-seen quotes that will make your communication more intriguing. Read it and reap."

—Sam Horn,
author of *POP! Create the Perfect Pitch, Title and Tagline for Anything*

"Allen, San Francisco Jollytologist®, has been making me happy in a variety of ways since I first met him. I love writing about him for the sheer joy of bringing his presence into my life and recalling all he has to say."

—Janet Gallin,
host of the talk show "Love Letters Live"

Readers praise Allen Klein:

"A couple of weeks ago I purchased a copy of your book, *Change Your Life*. My favorite quotes are uplifting, and I was eager to partake of your collection. I had no idea what an effect your book would have. Thanks for providing this book and inspiring so many people. The words you have collected have lifted our family's spirits. There are no words great enough to thank you for that..."

"But it's thanks to you and your book that I see these stars and am guided by them every day. And there's no words that I can use to express my gratitude. You've done something truly special by creating such a book. You saved my life. You really did! Thank you. You see, even though I know I'm not the first writing to say this, I just need to say 'Thank You' for creating such an inspiring book. I know there are hundreds of other inspiring quote books in the world, yet it was this particular book that helped to save my life years ago, and I'm always going to cherish it because of that..."

"I read your book, *Change Your Life*, and I realized every-thing will work out for the best and this truly did happen for a reason. I realized how lucky I was to be alive and what a miracle it was. In twenty years it's not going to matter who I graduated with, and this is going to make me stronger..."

"Writing to let you know I'm truly enjoying this book. I came across it by accident at the bookstore, where they had only one copy. I believe it was just sitting there waiting for me with its torn cover. I really needed this book at this time in my life. Thank you for sharing these wonderful uplifting quotes. I carry the book with me in my purse or always have it in my car..."

"You'll never know how your book has impacted my life. It was given to me as a gift a few years ago, and placed it on a shelf. Picked it up one day and have read it over & over. And I want to thank you from the bottom of my heart. I keep the quote taped on my kitchen cabinet, so I see it every day. Thank you again..."

words *of* love

Other Viva Editions books
by Allen Klein:

Change Your Life!: A Little Book of Big Ideas

Inspiration for a Lifetime:
Words of Wisdom, Delight and Possibility

The Art of Living Joyfully:
How to Be Happier Every Day of the Year

words *of* love

quotations *from the* heart

COMPILED BY
ALLEN KLEIN

FOREWORD BY
GREG GODEK

EDITIONS

Published in the United States by Viva Editions, an imprint of Cleis Press, Inc., 2246 Sixth Street, Berkeley, California 94710.

Printed in China.
Cover design: Scott Idleman/Blink & Shade Tree Greetings
Cover photograph: Christina Krutz/Getty Images
Text design: Frank Wiedemann & Shade Tree Greetings

Second Edition.
10 9 8 7 6 5 4 3 2 1

Hardcover ISBN: 978-1-936740-30-7
E-book ISBN: 978-1-936740-36-9

Library of Congress Cataloging-in-Publication Data

Words of love : quotations from the heart / compiled by Allen Klein ; foreword by Greg Godek. -- Second edition.
     pages cm
Includes index.
ISBN 978-1-936740-30-7
1. Love--Quotations, maxims, etc. I. Klein, Allen.
PN6084.L6W68 2012
081--dc23
                    2012037669

My gratitude and love to the higher power
who gave me talent
and to all those along my path
who helped nourish it.

CONTENTS

xxi

FOREWORD

xxiii

INTRODUCTION

1

LOVE MAKES THE WORLD GO 'ROUND:
WHAT IS LOVE?

19

LOVE IS A MANY-SPLENDORED THING:
FALLING IN LOVE

33

HELLO YOUNG LOVERS:
FIRST LOVE

39

I JUST CALLED TO SAY I LOVE YOU:
ROMANTIC LOVE

61

LOVE AND MARRIAGE:
LOVING COUPLES

79

M IS FOR THE MILLION THINGS SHE GAVE ME:
A MOTHER'S LOVE

89

I CAN'T GIVE YOU ANYTHING BUT LOVE, BABY:
LOVING YOURSELF

97

EMBRACEABLE YOU:
HUGS AND KISSES

117

LOVE POTION NUMBER NINE:
LOVE CONQUERS ALL

129

ALL YOU NEED IS LOVE:
UNCONDITIONAL LOVE

141

INDEX TO AUTHORS

149

ABOUT THE AUTHOR

FOREWORD

This little book that you hold so casually in your hands is worth about a million dollars. So you may want to hold onto it a bit more carefully. (And you may want to marvel at the miracle that this book costs less than twenty dollars!)

Why would I claim that *Words of Love* is worth a million dollars? Because it is coauthored by many of the brightest minds, the most compassionate people, and the most insightful thinkers that the human race has produced in the last 3,000 years.

How much would it be worth to hear the wisdom of Carl Jung, the observations of Albert Einstein, the musings of Henry David Thoreau, and the insights of Mother Teresa? What would you pay for a time machine that would allow you to travel back and listen to a lecture by Ralph Waldo Emerson, or walk along the Chinese countryside with Lau-Tzu, or have a conversation with Voltaire, or visit Charles Schulz's studio?

What would you pay for a ticket to attend the very first performance of William Shakespeare's *Romeo and Juliet*?

What would it be worth to talk with Woody Allen as he wrote the screenplay for *Annie Hall?* What would it be like to sit with James Thurber while he scribbled those insightfully droll relationship cartoons for *The New Yorker?*

What do you think the insights of Helen Keller—or the unknown author of *Corinthians*—are worth? Or the poetry of Elizabeth Barrett Browning—or Robert Frost? Or the paintings of Vincent van Gogh—or Pablo Picasso?

Through the magic of in-depth reading and careful selection of insightful passages, Allen Klein has gathered the wisdom of hundreds of wise men and women from ancient to modern times, as they express their feelings and observations about the single most important topic in the universe: Love.

These 500-plus quotations have been lovingly selected for you. Yes, you.

Enjoy,

Greg Godek
Author of the 3-million-copy bestseller *1001 Ways to be Romantic*

INTRODUCTION

One of the founders of the *Saturday Review of Literature,* Christopher Morley, once noted "if we all discovered that we had only five minutes left to say all that we wanted to say, every telephone booth would be occupied by people calling other people to stammer that they loved them."

This book is a reminder not to wait for those last moments.

Nearly all of the more than 500 quotations, from first love to unconditional love, illustrate just how powerful love can be. These insights can help bring more love to every aspect of your life or someone else's.

While compiling these quotations, their wisdom kept ringing in my ears and opened me up to both giving and receiving more love. I hope the words in this book do the same for you.

Allen Klein
San Francisco

True love defies time and distance.

ANONYMOUS

Love Makes the World Go 'Round

What is Love?

Love doesn't make the world go 'round.
Love is what makes the ride worthwhile.
FRANKLIN P. JONES

Love is the master key that opens the gates of happiness.
OLIVER WENDELL HOLMES

Love is heaven and heaven is love.
SIR WALTER SCOTT

Love should be a tree whose roots are deep in the earth,
but whose branches extend into heaven.
BERTRAND RUSSELL

Love is patient, love is kind. It does not envy, it does not
boast, it is not proud. It is not rude, it is not self-seeking,
it is not easily angered, it keeps no record of wrongs.
Love does not delight in evil but rejoices with the truth. It
always protects, always trusts, always hopes,
always perseveres.
1 CORINTHIANS 13:4-7

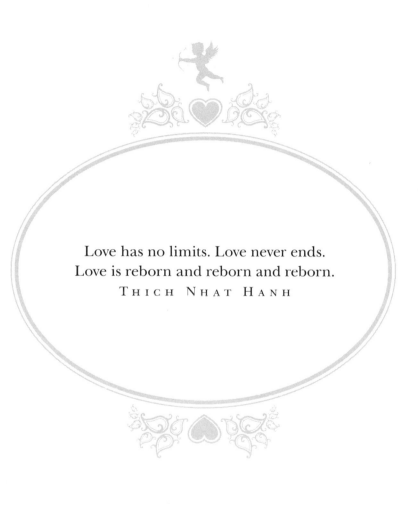

Love has no limits. Love never ends.
Love is reborn and reborn and reborn.

THICH NHAT HANH

Love is never lost. If not reciprocated it will flow back
and soften and purify the heart.
WASHINGTON IRVING

Love is what we were born with.
Fear is what we learned here.
MARIANNE WILLIAMSON

Love has no age, as it is always renewing.
BLAISE PASCAL

Love is like infinity: You can't have more or less infinity,
and you can't compare two things to see if they're
"equally infinite." Infinity just is, and that's the way I
think love is, too.
FRED ROGERS

Love is an energy—
it can neither be created nor destroyed.
It just is and always will be, giving meaning to life and
direction to goodness… Love will never die.
BRYCE COURTENAY

Love is the immortal flow of energy that nourishes,
extends and preserves. Its eternal goal is life.
SMILEY BLANTON

Love is a mighty power, a great and complete good.
Love alone lightens every burden,
and makes the rough places smooth.
THOMAS À KEMPIS

Without love our life is…a ship without a rudder…
like a body without a soul.
SHOLEM ALEICHEM

I define love thus: the will to extend one's self
for the purpose of nurturing one's own
or another's spiritual growth.
M. SCOTT PECK

The essence of love is creative companionship,
the fulfillment of one life by another.
JOHN ERSKINE

Love is but the discovery of ourselves in others,
and the delight in the recognition.
ALEXANDER SMITH

Love is the experience of others as "us,"
and not separately as him, her or them.
KEN KEYES, JR.

Love is a game that two can play and both win.
EVA GABOR

Love is the only game
that is not called on account of darkness.
ANONYMOUS

When the satisfaction or security of another person
becomes as significant to one as is
one's own satisfaction or security,
then the state of love exists.
HARRY STACK SULLIVAN

A lady of forty-seven who has been married twenty-seven
years and has six children knows what love really is and
once described it for me like this: "Love is what you've
been through with somebody."

JAMES THURBER

Love is when I am concerned with your relationship with
your own life rather than with your relationship to mine.

STEWART EMORY

Love is…the ability and willingness to allow those that
you care for to be what they choose for themselves,
without any insistence that they satisfy you.

WAYNE DYER

Love is an act of endless forgiveness,
a tender look which becomes a habit.

PETER USTINOV

Love is the free exercise of choice. Two people love each
other only when they are quite capable of living without
each other but *choose*
to live with each other.

M. SCOTT PECK

Love is when two people
who care for each other get confused.
BOB SCHNEIDER

What is irritating about love is that
it is a crime that requires an accomplice.
CHARLES BAUDELAIRE

Love is said to be blind, but I know lots of fellows in love
who can see twice as much in their sweethearts as I can.
JOSH BILLINGS

Love is not blind—it sees more, not less.
But because it sees more,
it is willing to see less.
JULIUS GORDON

Love is always open arms.
If you close your arms about love
you will find that you are left holding only yourself.
LEO BUSCAGLIA

Love is an irresistible desire to be irresistibly desired.
ROBERT FROST

Love is like quicksilver in the hand.
Leave the fingers open, and it stays.
Clutch it, and it darts away.

DOROTHY PARKER

Love is, above all, the gift of oneself.
JEAN ANOUILH

Love is like an hourglass,
with the heart filling up as the brain empties.
JULES RENARD

Love is an infusion of intense feeling, a fine madness that
makes you drunk, and when one is in love, life can be a
succession of free falls while working without a net.
MERLE SHAIN

Love is friendship set on fire.
JEREMY TAYLOR

Love is a fire. But whether it is going to warm your
hearth or burn down your house, you can never tell.
JOAN CRAWFORD

Love is a mystery which, when solved, evaporates.
NED ROREM

What a silly thing love is! It is not half as useful as logic,
for it does not prove anything and it is always telling one
things that are not going to happen, and making one
believe things that are not true.

OSCAR WILDE

Love is an endless mystery,
for it has nothing else to explain it.

RABINDRANATH TAGORE

Love is much nicer to be in than an automobile accident,
a tight girdle, a higher tax bracket or a holding pattern
over Philadelphia.

JUDITH VIORST

If love is the answer, could you rephrase the question?

LILY TOMLIN

I know what love is:
Tracy and Hepburn, Bogart and Bacall,
Romeo and Juliet, Jackie and John and Marilyn.

IAN SHOALES

Everyone admits that love is wonderful and necessary,
yet no one can agree on what it is.
D I A N E   A C K E R M A N

Love betters what is best.
W I L L I A M   W O R D S W O R T H

Love conceals all of one's faults.
I T A L I A N   P R O V E R B

Love often makes a fool of the cleverest man,
and as often gives cleverness to the most foolish.
F R E N C H   P R O V E R B

Love seeks one thing only: The good of the one loved.
It leaves all the other secondary effects to take care of
themselves. Love, therefore, is its own reward.
T H O M A S   M E R T O N

Love understands love: It needs no talk.
F R A N C E S   R .   H A V E R G A L

Love feels no burden, thinks nothing of trouble
and attempts what is above its strength.

THOMAS À KEMPIS

To love someone deeply gives you strength.
Being loved by someone deeply gives you courage.

LAO-TZU

Life has taught us that love does not consist in gazing at
each other but in looking outward together
in the same direction.

ANTOINE DE SAINT-EXUPÉRY

We are shaped and fashioned by what we love.

JOHANN WOLFGANG VON GOETHE

To love is to suffer. To avoid suffering one must not love.
But then one suffers from not loving. Therefore to love
is to suffer, not to love is to suffer. To suffer is to suffer.
To be happy is to love. To be happy then is to suffer. But
suffering makes one unhappy. Therefore, to be unhappy
one must love, or love to suffer, or suffer from too much
happiness. I hope you're getting this down.

WOODY ALLEN

Without love the world itself would not survive.
LOPE DE VEGA

Love cannot save life from death;
but it can fulfill life's purpose.
ARNOLD TOYNBEE

Paradise is always where love dwells.
JEAN PAUL RICHTER

Only through love
can we attain to communion with God.
ALBERT SCHWEITZER

In our life there is a single color,
as on an artist's palette,
which provides the meaning of life and art.
It is the color of love.
MARC CHAGALL

Love is something eternal;
the aspect may change, but not the essence.
VINCENT VAN GOGH

Love is a canvas furnished by Nature
and embroidered by imagination.
VOLTAIRE

Love is the only gold.
ALFRED, LORD TENNYSON

There is nothing in the world so sweet as love.
ITALIAN PROVERB

What does love look like? It has the hands to help others.
It has the feet to hasten to the poor and needy. It has eyes
to see misery and want. It has the ears to hear the sighs
and sorrows of men. That is what love looks like.
SAINT AUGUSTINE

Harmony is pure love, for love is a concerto.
LOPE DE VEGA

Love is friendship set to music.
E. JOSEPH COSSMAN

Love is like a violin. The music may stop now and then,
but the strings remain forever.
JUNE MASTERS BACHER

Love is a letter on pink stationery.
CHARLES SCHULZ

What is love? It is the morning and the evening star.
SINCLAIR LEWIS

Love is the light you can see by.
BESS STREETER ALDRICH

Love is the poetry of the senses.
HONORÉ DE BALZAC

Love is the greatest beautifier in the universe.
MAY CHRISTIE

Love is no hot-house flower,
but a wild plant, born of a wet night,
born of an hour of sunshine; sprung from wild seed,
blown along the road by a wild wind.
JOHN GALSWORTHY

Life is the flower for which love is the honey.
VICTOR HUGO

Love is a fruit in season at all times,
and within reach of every hand.
MOTHER TERESA

Love is the greatest refreshment in life.
PABLO PICASSO

Love is the food of the universe. It is the most important
ingredient in life. Children go towards love, they thrive
on love and grow on love, and would die without it.
SANAYA ROMAN

Love is sharing your popcorn.
CHARLES SCHULZ

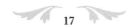

Love, like a chicken salad or restaurant hash, must be taken with blind faith or it loses its flavor.

HELEN ROWLAND

Love is sweet, but tastes better with bread.

YIDDISH PROVERB

Love Is a Many-Splendored Thing

Falling in Love

To love and be loved is to feel the sun from both sides.
DAVID VISCOTT

You'll never be happy if you can't figure out
that loving people is all there is.
And that it's more important to love than be loved.
Because that is when you feel love, by loving somebody.
GWYNETH PALTROW

The simple but observable fact is that the more you love,
the more you are able to love.
JOYCE BROTHERS

Love, and you shall be loved.
RALPH WALDO EMERSON

Love is not getting, but giving. It is sacrifice. And sacrifice
is glorious! I have no patience with women who measure
and weigh their love like a country doctor dispensing
capsules. If a man is worth loving at all, he is worth loving
generously, even recklessly.
MARIE DRESSLER

The one thing we never give enough of is love.

HENRY MILLER

If you give your life as a wholehearted response to love,
then love will wholeheartedly respond to you.
MARIANNE WILLIAMSON

Saving love doesn't bring any interest.
MAE WEST

Only love can be divided endlessly and still not diminish.
ANNE MORROW LINDBERGH

You can offer your love completely to hundreds of people
and still retain the same love you had originally. It is like
knowledge. The wise man can teach all he knows and
when he's through he'll still know
all that he has taught.
LEO BUSCAGLIA

I know of only one duty, and that is to love.
ALBERT CAMUS

There is more pleasure in loving than in being loved.
THOMAS FULLER

All that we love deeply becomes a part of us.

HELEN KELLER

Tell me whom you love, and I will tell you what you are.

ARSÈNE HOUSSAYE

Listen to no one who tells you how to love. Your love is like no other, and that is what makes it beautiful.

PAUL WILLIAMS

You will find as you look back upon your life that the moments when you have truly lived are the moments when you have done things in the spirit of love.

HENRY DRUMMOND

You don't have to go looking for love when it's where you come from.

WERNER ERHARD

The love we desire is already within us.

A COURSE IN MIRACLES

If you ever expect to be loved,
you must reveal who you are.

LEO BUSCAGLIA

When you really want love you will find it waiting for you.
OSCAR WILDE

When love comes it comes without effort,
like perfect weather.
HELEN YGLESIAS

We can never at any time absorb more love
than we're ready for.
MIGNON McLAUGHLIN

I think that when we look for love courageously, it reveals
itself, and we wind up attracting even more love. If one
person really wants us, everyone does. But if we're alone,
we become even more alone.
PAULO COELHO

The supreme happiness in life
is the conviction that we are loved.
VICTOR HUGO

Love doesn't drop on you unexpectedly; you have to give
off signals, sort of like an amateur radio operator.
HELEN GURLEY BROWN

To love is to receive a glimpse of heaven.
KAREN SUNDE

There is no surprise more magical than the surprise of
being in love. It is God's finger on man's shoulder.
CHARLES MORGAN

We want to be rich, to be admired, to eat like a horse
and be skinny as a snake. To have small children ask for
our autographs, to be on terrific medications that make
us calm and witty and sexy. To sing Irving Berlin and
Gershwin and Porter at the Oak Room and be described
in the *Times* as "luminous." But in the absence of all that,
it's enough to be loved.
GARRISON KEILLOR

To be loved, be lovable.

OVID

When love is good it can make you fly. Winning it is
worth the risk. People fall in love and glow for weeks.

GEORGE DAVIS

Gravitation cannot be held responsible
for people falling in love.

ALBERT EINSTEIN

Falling in love consists merely
in uncorking the imagination
and bottling the common sense.

HELEN ROWLAND

To fall in love
you have to be in the state of mind for it to take,
like a disease.

NANCY MITFORD

To be in love is merely to be in a state of perceptual anesthesia—to mistake an ordinary young man for a Greek god or an ordinary young woman for a goddess.

H. L. MENCKEN

Romantic love is mental illness. But it's a pleasurable one.

FRAN LEBOWITZ

It is difficult to know at what moment love begins; it is less difficult to know that it has begun.

HENRY WADSWORTH LONGFELLOW

A guy knows he's in love when he loses interest in his car for a couple of days.

TIM ALLEN

A successful marriage requires falling in love many times, always with the same person.

GERMAINE GREER

Any time that is not spent on love is wasted.

TORQUATO TASSO

Love doesn't just sit there, like a stone; it has to be made, like bread, remade all the time, made new.

URSULA LE GUIN

There is always something left to love.
And if you ain't learned that, you ain't learned nothing.
LORRAINE HANSBERRY

Love affairs are the only real education in life.
MARLENE DIETRICH

There is no remedy for love but to love more.
HENRY DAVID THOREAU

That is the true season of love,
when we believe that we alone can love,
that no one could ever have loved so before us
and that no one will love in the same way after us.
JOHANN WOLFGANG VON GOETHE

The weather is always fair when people are in love.
ITALIAN PROVERB

I was nauseous and tingly all over.
I was either in love or I had smallpox.
WOODY ALLEN

To fall in love is awfully simple,
but to fall out of love is simply awful.

ANONYMOUS

One does not fall "in" or "out" of love.
One grows in love.

LEO BUSCAGLIA

Being in love is experiencing a person's essence
and expression of that essence,
and being unwilling for the other person
not to express it.

STEWART EMORY

The meeting of two personalities
is like the contact of two chemical substances:
If there is any reaction, both are transformed.

CARL JUNG

There is no disguise
which can hide love for long where it exists,
or simulate it where it does not.

FRANÇOIS DUC DE LA ROCHEFOUCAULD

Where love does not exist, plant it and it will grow.
SAN JUAN DE LA CRUZ

It doesn't matter who you love or how you love,
but that you love.
ROD McKUEN

Hello Young Lovers

First Love

First romance, first love,
is something so special to all of us,
both emotionally and physically,
that it touches our lives
and enriches them forever.

ROSEMARY ROGERS

One always returns to one's first loves.

HENRI ÉTIENNE

How on earth are you ever going to explain in terms of
chemistry and physics so important a biological phenom-
enon as first love?

ALBERT EINSTEIN

Love is so very timid when 'tis new.

LORD BYRON

The magic of first love is our ignorance
that it can ever end.

BENJAMIN DISRAELI

The first sigh of love is the last of wisdom.
ANTOINE BRET

We are all mortal until the first kiss
and the second glass of wine.
EDUARDO GALEANO

How delicious is the winning of a kiss at love's beginning.
THOMAS CAMPBELL

There's nothing half so sweet in life
as love's young dream.
CLEMENT C. MOORE

First love is only a little foolishness and a lot of curiosity.
GEORGE BERNARD SHAW

Young love needs dangers and barriers to nourish it.
GEORGE SAND

When a couple of young people strongly devoted to each
other commence to eat onions, it is safe to pronounce
them engaged.
JAMES MONTGOMERY BAILEY

Teenagers don't know what love is. They have mixed up ideas. They go for a drive, and the boy runs out of gas, and they smooch a little and the girl says she loves him. That isn't love. Love is when you are married twenty-five years, smooching in your living room, and he runs out of gas and she says she still loves him. That's love.

NORM CROSBY

Young love is a flame; very pretty, often very hot and fierce, but still only light and flickering. The love of the older and disciplined heart is as coals, deep-burning, unquenchable.

HENRY WARD BEECHER

The heart that loves is always young.

GREEK PROVERB

A boy's love comes from a full heart;
a man's is more often the result of a full stomach.

JEROME K. JEROME

Love and eggs are best when they are fresh.

RUSSIAN PROVERB

I Just Called to Say I Love You

Romantic Love

How do I love thee? Let me count the ways.
I love thee to the depth and breadth and height
My soul can reach.

ELIZABETH BARRETT BROWNING

Brevity may be the soul of wit, but not when someone's
saying "I love you." When someone's saying "I love you,"
he always ought to give a lot of details: Like, why does he
love you? And, when and where did he first begin to love
you? Favorable comparisons with all the other women he
ever loved are also welcome. And even though he insists
it would take forever to count the ways in which he loves
you, let him start counting.

JUDITH VIORST

I love you as New Englanders love pie!

DON MARQUIS

How Do I Love Thee?
I love you more than yesterday, less than tomorrow.

EDMOND ROSTAND

I love you no matter what you do,
but do you have to do so much of it?
JEAN ILLSLEY CLARKE

I love you, not only for what you are,
but for what I am when I am with you.
ROY CROFT

All that I love loses half its pleasure
if you are not there to share it.
CLARA ORTEGA

All that you are, all that I owe to you,
justifies my love, and nothing, not even you,
would keep me from adoring you.
MARQUIS DE LAFAYETTE

Ask the child why it is born;
ask the flower why it blossoms, ask the sun why it shines.
I love you because I must love you.
GEORGE UPTON

If I know what love is, it is because of you.

HERMANN HESSE

"Love, shmove," Papa used to say, "I love blintzes; Did I
marry one?"
SAM LEVENSON

In love the paradox occurs
that two beings become one and yet remain two.
ERICH FROMM

For one human being to love another;
that is perhaps the most difficult of all our tasks,
the ultimate, the last test and proof,
the work for which all other work is but preparation.
RAINER MARIA RILKE

There is a universal truth that I have found in my work.
Everybody longs to be loved. And the greatest thing we
can do is let somebody know that they are loved and
capable of loving.
FRED ROGERS

When one is truly in love,
one not only says it, but shows it.
HENRY WADSWORTH LONGFELLOW

It is a curious thought, but it is only when you see people looking ridiculous that you realize just how much you love them.

AGATHA CHRISTIE

We are told that people stay in love because of chemistry, or because they remain intrigued with each other, because of many kindnesses, because of luck... But part of it has got to be forgiveness and gratefulness. The understanding that, so, you're no bargain, but you love and you are loved. Anyway.

ELLEN GOODMAN

And what do all the great words come to in the end, but that?—
I love you—I am at rest with you—I have come home.

DOROTHY L. SAYERS

From the moment we walk out the door until we come back home our sensibilities are so assaulted by the world at large that we have to soak up as much love as we can get, simply to arm ourselves. It's like going to the gas station for a refill. We humans need to hear "I love you" and we need to hear it as often as we can.

PATTY DUKE

The greatest weakness of most humans
is their hesitancy to tell others how much they love them
while they're still alive.

ORLANDO A. BATTISTA

In order to love simply,
it is necessary to know how to show love.

FYODOR DOSTOEVSKY

If you love somebody, tell them.

ROD McKUEN

Romance is the icing but love is the cake.

ANONYMOUS

Love is a valentine with lace all around the edges.

CHARLES SCHULZ

In a great romance,
each person plays a part the other really likes.

ELIZABETH ASHLEY

Story writers say that love is concerned only with young
people, and the excitement and glamour of romance
end at the altar. How blind they are. The best romance
is inside marriage; the finest love stories come after the
wedding, not before.

IRVING STONE

My wife is really sentimental.
One Valentine's Day I gave her a ring, and to this day,
she has never forgotten those three little words
that were engraved inside—Made in Taiwan!
LEOPOLD FECHTNER

In real love you want the other person's good.
In romantic love you want the other person.
MARGARET ANDERSON

There is nothing better for the spirit or the body
than a love affair.
It elevates the thoughts
and flattens the stomachs.
BARBARA HOWER

The heart has reasons that reason does not understand.
JACQUES-BÉNIGNE BOSSUET

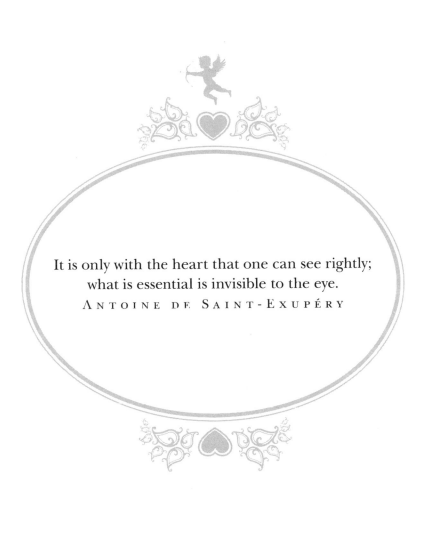

It is only with the heart that one can see rightly;
what is essential is invisible to the eye.

ANTOINE DE SAINT-EXUPÉRY

Many a man does not find his heart
until he has lost his head.

FRIEDRICH NIETZSCHE

A good heart is better than all the heads in the world.

EDWARD BULWER-LYTTON

What the heart knows today,
the head will understand tomorrow.

JAMES STEPHENS

There is no feeling in a human heart which exists in that
heart alone—which is not, in some form or degree, in
every heart.

GEORGE MACDONALD

What comes from the heart, goes to the heart.

SAMUEL TAYLOR COLERIDGE

The human heart, at whatever age, opens only to the
heart that opens in return.

MARIA EDGEWORTH

For every beauty there is an eye somewhere to see it.
For every truth there is an ear somewhere to hear it.
For every love there is a heart somewhere to receive it.

I V A N   P A N I N

So long as the memory of certain beloved friends
lives in my heart,
I shall say that life is good.

H E L E N   K E L L E R

Absence makes the heart grow fonder.

T H O M A S   H A Y N E S   B A Y L Y

They say absence makes the heart grow fonder,
so I figure that's why my boyfriend moved.

C H R I S T Y   M U R P H Y

Love is space and time measured by the heart.

M A R C E L   P R O U S T

If you have much, give of your wealth;
if you have little, give of your heart.

A R A B   P R O V E R B

Without a rich heart, wealth is an ugly beggar.
RALPH WALDO EMERSON

Accept the things to which fate binds you, and love the
people with whom fate brings you together, but do so
with all your heart.
MARCUS AURELIUS

If you find it in your heart to care for somebody else,
you will have succeeded.
MAYA ANGELOU

The moment you have in your heart this extraordinary
thing called love and feel the depth, the delight, the
ecstasy of it, you will discover
that for you the world is transformed.
J. KRISHNAMURTI

Love wasn't put in your heart to stay,
Love isn't love till you give it away.
ANONYMOUS

A loving heart is the truest wisdom.
CHARLES DICKENS

Your heart is greater than your wounds.
HENRI J. M. NOUWEN

Nobody has ever measured, not even poets,
how much the heart can hold.
ZELDA FITZGERALD

When you begin to touch your heart or let your heart be
touched, you begin to discover that it's bottomless, that it
doesn't have any resolution, that this heart is huge, vast,
and limitless.
PEMA CHÖDRÖN

Love makes all hard hearts gentle.
GEORGE HERBERT

When the seeds of brotherly love
take root in the hearts of people, wars will cease.
PARAMAHANSA YOGANANDA

I will make love my greatest weapon and none on who I
call can defend against its force… My love will melt all
hearts liken to the sun whose rays soften the coldest day.
OG MANDINO

Keep love in your heart. A life without it
is like a sunless garden when the flowers are dead. The
consciousness of loving and being loved
brings a warmth and richness to life
that nothing else can bring.

OSCAR WILDE

Occasionally in life there are those moments of
unutterable fulfillment which cannot be completely
explained by those symbols called words.
Their meanings can only be articulated
by the inaudible language of the heart.

MARTIN LUTHER KING, JR.

Give all to love; obey thy heart.

RALPH WALDO EMERSON

Let those love now who never loved before;
Let those who always loved, now love the more.

THOMAS PARNELL

All the world loves a lover.

RALPH WALDO EMERSON

We are most alive when we're in love.
JOHN UPDIKE

I should like to call you by all the endearing epithets,
and yet I can find no lovelier word than the simple word
"dear," but there is a particular way of saying it. My dear
one, then, I have wept for joy
to think that you are mine.
ROBERT SCHUMANN

If you love 'em in the morning with their eyes full of
crust; if you love 'em at night with their hair full of
rollers, chances are, you're in love.
MILES DAVIS

Two souls with but a single thought,
Two hearts that beat as one.
FRIEDRICH HALM

When you're in love,
it's the most glorious two-and-a-half days
of your life.
RICHARD LEWIS

If you can stay in love for more than two years,
you're on something.
FRAN LEBOWITZ

There is only one situation I can think of in which men
and women make an effort to read better than they
usually do. When they are in love and reading a love
letter, they read for all they are worth. They read every
word three ways; they read between the lines and in the
margins... Then, if never before or after, they read.
MORTIMER J. ADLER

A love letter begins by your not knowing
what you are going to say,
and ends by your not knowing
what you have said.
ANONYMOUS

What a woman says to her lover
should be written on air or swift water.
CATULLUS

A woman knows the face of the man she loves
like a sailor knows the open sea.

HONORÉ DE BALZAC

Women prefer men who have something tender about
them—especially the legal kind.

KAY INGRAM

There is a place you can touch a woman
that will drive her crazy.
Her heart.

MELANIE GRIFFITH

When a young man complains
that a young lady has no heart,
it is pretty certain that she has his.

GEORGE DENNISON PRENTICE

One makes mistakes: that is life.
But it is never quite a mistake to have loved.

ROMAIN ROLLAND

Men always want to be a woman's first love—
women like to be a man's last romance.

OSCAR WILDE

It is better to have loved and lost,
than never to have loved at all.
ALFRED, LORD TENNYSON

If you believe yourself unfortunate, because you have
loved and lost, perish the thought. One who has loved
truly, can never lose entirely.
NAPOLEON HILL

The quarrels of lovers are like summer storms. Everything is more beautiful when they have passed.
SUZANNE NECKER

Anyone can be passionate,
but it takes real lovers to be silly.
ROSE FRANKEN

Among those whom I like or admire,
I can find no common denominator,
but among those whom I love, I can:
All of them make me laugh.

W. H. AUDEN

Lovers can live on kisses and cool water.

FRENCH PROVERB

Love and Marriage

Loving Couples

To have and to hold from this day forward,
for better for worse,
for richer for poorer, in sickness and in health,
to love and to cherish, till death us do part.
THE BOOK OF COMMON PRAYER

Marriage is like a flourishing garden,
alive with rich soil, colorful blooms,
delightful fragrances and pleasant surprises—
and thorns, beetles, weeds, and perhaps a mole.
NANCY McCORD

Marriage is like twirling a baton, turning a handspring
or eating with chopsticks; it looks easy until you try it.
HELEN ROWLAND

Marriage is not a ritual or an end. It is a long, intricate,
intimate dance together and nothing matters more than
your own sense of balance and your choice of partner.
AMY BLOOM

Marriage resembles a pair of shears,
so joined that they cannot be separated;
often moving in opposite directions,
yet always punishing anyone who comes between them.
SYDNEY SMITH

Marriage is a woman's hair net
tangled in a man's spectacles
on top of a dresser drawer.
DON HEROLD

Marriage is like vitamins:
We supplement each other's
minimum daily requirements.
KATHY MOHNKE

A marriage is like a long trip in a tiny rowboat: If one passenger starts to rock the boat, the other has to steady it; otherwise they will go to the bottom together.

DAVID ROBERT REUBEN

Marriage is not just spiritual communion and passionate embraces; marriage is also three-meals-a-day and remembering to carry out the trash.

JOYCE BROTHERS

Marriage is a lot like the army, everyone complains, but you'd be surprised at the large number that re-enlist.

JAMES GARNER

It (marriage) may be compared to a cage, the birds without try desperately to get in, and those within try desperately to get out.

MICHEL DE MONTAIGNE

Marriage is a good deal like a circus: There is not as much in it as is represented in the advertising.

EDGAR WATSON HOWE

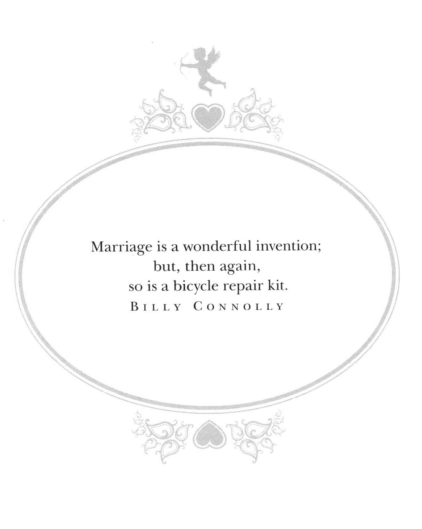

Marriage is a wonderful invention;
but, then again,
so is a bicycle repair kit.
BILLY CONNOLLY

Marriage is our last, best chance to grow up.
JOSEPH BARTH

Coupling... Two people holding each other up like flying
buttresses. Two people depending on each other and
babying each other and defending each other against
the world outside. Sometimes it was worth all the disad-
vantages of marriage just to have that: One friend in an
indifferent world.
ERICA JONG

A marriage makes of two fractional lives a whole;
it gives to two purposeless lives a work,
and doubles the strength of each to perform it;
it gives to two questioning natures a reason for living,
and something to live for.
MARK TWAIN

I love being married...
It's so great to find that one special person
you want to annoy for the rest of your life.

RITA RUDNER

You and your husband are alone in a cabin for the first
time since your marriage. He is nibbling on your ear. Do
you (a) nibble back or (b) tell him the toilet is running?

ERMA BOMBECK

Marrying a man is like buying something you've been
admiring for a long time in a shop window. You may love
it when you get it home, but it doesn't always go with
everything else.

JEAN KERR

I want a man who's kind and understanding.
Is that too much to ask of a millionaire?

ZSA ZSA GABOR

There is only one thing for a man to do who is married
to a woman who enjoys spending money, and that is to
enjoy earning it.

EDGAR WATSON HOWE

67

An archaeologist is the best husband
any woman can have;
the older she gets,
the more interested he is in her.
AGATHA CHRISTIE

My parents want me to get married. They don't care who
anymore as long as he doesn't have a pierced ear, that's
all they care about. I think men who have a pierced ear
are better prepared for marriage. They've experienced
pain and bought jewelry.

RITA RUDNER

By all means marry.
If you get a good wife, you'll be happy.
If you get a bad one, you'll become a philosopher.

SOCRATES

What's the best way to have your husband remember your
anniversary? Get married on his birthday.

CINDY GARNER

A girl must marry for love,
and keep on marrying until she finds it.

ZSA ZSA GABOR

One good reason to get married is you'll always have
someone to blame when you can't find your keys.

JOHN LOUIS ANDERSON

I…chose my wife, as she did her wedding gown,
not for a fine glossy surface, but such qualities as would
wear well.

OLIVER GOLDSMITH

People shop for a bathing suit with more care than they
do a husband or wife. The rules are the same. Look for
something you'll feel comfortable wearing. Allow for
room to grow.

ERMA BOMBECK

Women hope men will change after marriage but they
don't; men hope women won't change but they do.

BETTINA ARNDT

What's the difference between a boyfriend
and a husband?
About 30 pounds.

CINDY GARNER

Instead of getting married again,
I'm going to find a woman
I don't like and just give her a house.

ROD STEWART

The real act of marriage takes place in the heart, not in
the ballroom or church or synagogue. It's a choice you
make—not just on your wedding day, but over and over
again—and that choice is reflected in the way you treat
your husband or wife.

BARBARA DE ANGELIS

I would like to have engraved inside every wedding band,
"Be kind to one another." This is the golden rule of
marriage and the secret
of making love last through the years.

RUDOLPH RAY

A successful marriage is an edifice
that must be rebuilt every day.

ANDRÉ MAUROIS

Remember that a good marriage is like a campfire.
Both grow cold if left unattended.

H. JACKSON BROWN, JR.

Marriages we regard as the happiest
are those in which each of the partners believes
that he or she got the best of it.

SYDNEY J. HARRIS

A good marriage is at least 80 percent good luck in
finding the right person at the right time.
The rest is trust.

NANETTE NEWMAN

There is no greater risk, perhaps, than matrimony,
but there is nothing happier than a happy marriage.

BENJAMIN DISRAELI

There is no more lovely, friendly and charming relationship, communion or company than a good marriage.

MARTIN LUTHER

Never forget
the nine most important words of any marriage:
1. I love you. 2. You are beautiful. 3. Please forgive me.

H. JACKSON BROWN, JR.

People are always asking couples whose marriage has
endured at least a quarter of a century for their secret
for success. Actually, it is no secret at all. I am a forgiving
woman. Long ago, I forgave my husband for not being
Paul Newman.

ERMA BOMBECK

The best thing that can happen to a couple married
for fifty years or more is that they
both grow nearsighted together.

LINDA FITERMAN

Love seems the swiftest,
but it is the slowest of all growths.
No man or woman really knows what perfect love is
until they have been married a quarter of a century.

MARK TWAIN

After fifteen years of marriage,
my wife wants us to recommit our vows.
As a man, I don't understand her need to get married
again. We've got our toaster, let's move on.

ROBERT G. LEE

My wife Mary and I have been married for
forty-seven years, and not once have we had an
argument serious enough to consider divorce; murder,
yes, but divorce, never.

JACK BENNY

The secret to happy marriages,
relationships and terrific friendships includes
the ability to be playful and childlike.

DALE ANDERSON

Sexiness wears thin after a while,
but to be married to a man who makes you laugh every
day, ah, now that's a real treat.

JOANNE WOODWARD

We cannot really love anybody
with whom we never laugh.

AGNES REPPLIER

I want to make my wife laugh more.
Laughter engenders love.

RABBI SHMULEY BOTEACH

Some people ask the secret of our long marriage.
We take time to go to a restaurant two times a week.
A little candlelight, dinner, music and dancing.
She goes Tuesdays. I go Fridays.

HENNY YOUNGMAN

Before marriage the three little words are, "I love you";
after marriage they are, "Let's eat out."

ANONYMOUS

Through all the years of my marriage,
my love for Camille,
like my stomach, has steadily grown.

BILL COSBY

A good marriage is like a casserole,
only those responsible for it really know what goes in it.
ANONYMOUS

A long marriage is two people trying to dance a duet
and two solos at the same time.
ANNE TAYLOR FLEMING

The only thing wrong with marriage
is not seeing enough of each other.
EARL RUSSELL

A happy marriage is a long conversation
which always seems too short.
ANDRÉ MAUROIS

The wonderful thing about marriage is that you are the
most important person in someone else's life. If you
don't come home some evening, there is someone who is
going to go out looking for you.
JOYCE BROTHERS

Marriage should be a duet—
when one sings, the other claps.

JOE MURRAY

Take each other for better or worse but not for granted.
ARLENE DAHL

Chains do not hold a marriage together. It is threads,
hundreds of tiny threads, which sew people together
through the years.
SIMONE SIGNORET

The great secret of successful marriage
is to treat all disasters as incidents
and none of the incidents as disasters.
HAROLD NICOLSON

The secret of a happy marriage remains a secret.
HENNY YOUNGMAN

*M Is for The Million Things
She Gave Me*

A Mother's Love

Nothing's better than a mother's love.
AFRICAN PROVERB

There is no friendship, no love,
like that of the mother for the child.
HENRY WARD BEECHER

The greatest love is a mother's; then comes a dog's;
then comes a sweetheart's.
POLISH PROVERB

A mother's love for her child is like nothing else in the
world. It knows no law, no pity; it dares all things and
crushes down remorselessly
all that stands in its path.
AGATHA CHRISTIE

A mother's love perceives no impossibilities.
BENJAMIN HENRY PADDOCK

A mother's heart is a baby's most beautiful dwelling.
ED DUSSAULT

There is no other closeness in human life
like the closeness between a mother and her
baby—chronologically, physically,
and spiritually they are just a few heartbeats
away from being the same person.

SUSAN CHEEVER

Making the decision to have a child—it's momentous. It is to decide forever to have your heart go walking around outside your body.

E L I Z A B E T H   S T O N E

The heart of a mother is a deep abyss at the bottom of which you will always find forgiveness.

H O N O R É   D E   B A L Z A C

For me, motherhood has been the one true, great, and wholly successful romance. It is the only love I have known that is expansive and that could have stretched to contain with equal passion more than one object.

I R M A   K U R T Z

When you are a mother, you are never really alone in your thoughts. A mother always has to think twice, once for herself and once for her child.

S O P H I A   L O R E N

A mother is a person who, seeing there are only four
pieces of pie for five people, promptly announces she
never did care for pie.

TENNEVA JORDAN

I was not a classic mother. But my kids were never palmed
off to boarding school. So, I didn't bake cookies. You can
buy cookies, but you can't buy love.

RAQUEL WELCH

The mother loves her child most divinely, not when she
surrounds him with comfort and anticipates his wants,
but when she resolutely holds him to the highest stan-
dards and is content with nothing less than his best.

HAMILTON WRIGHT MABIE

No matter how old a mother is, she still watches her
middle-aged children for signs of improvement.

FLORIDA SCOTT-MAXWELL

The child who acts unlovable is the child
who most needs to be loved.

CATHY RINDNER TEMPELSMAN

You have to love your children unselfishly.
That's hard, but it's the only way.

BARBARA BUSH

Can we love our children when they are homely,
awkward, unkempt, flaunting the styles and friendships
we don't approve of, when they fail to be the best,
the brightest, the most accomplished at school or
even at home? Can we be there when their world has
fallen apart and only we can restore their faith
and confidence in life?

NEIL KURSHAN

A baby is born with a need to be loved—
and never outgrows it.

FRANK A. CLARK

The more love you give your children, the more love you
are helping them to create inside themselves. Think of
love as a basic right of your kids. Give it away freely, and it
will come back a thousand fold.

STEPHANIE MARSTON

Mother's love is peace. It need not be acquired,
it need not be deserved.

ERICH FROMM

I actually remember feeling delight, at two o'clock in the
morning, when the baby woke for this feed, because I so
longed to have another look at him.

MARGARET DRABBLE

A mother doesn't give a damn about your looks.
She thinks you are beautiful anyway.

MARION C. GARRETTY

Loving a baby is a circular business,
a kind of feedback loop.
The more you give the more you get
and the more you get
the more you feel like giving.

PENELOPE LEACH

Give a little love to a child, and you get a great deal back.

JOHN RUSKIN

Cherishing children is the mark of a civilized society.

JOAN GANZ COONEY

My best creation is my children.
DIANE VON FURSTENBERG

If you can't hold children in your arms,
please hold them in your heart.
CLARA HALE

My mother loved children—
she would have given anything if I had been one.
GROUCHO MARX

Some are kissing mothers and some are scolding
mothers, but it is love just the same, and most mothers
kiss and scold together.
PEARL S. BUCK

The only thing worth stealing
is a kiss from a sleeping child.
JOE HOULDSWORTH

We say "I love you" to our children, but it's not enough.
Maybe that's why mothers hug and hold and rock and
kiss and pat.
JOAN MCINTOSH

Have you hugged your child today?
SLOGAN

I Can't Give You Anything but Love, Baby

Self-Love

I celebrate myself, and sing myself.
WALT WHITMAN

Have you hugged yourself today?
ANONYMOUS

To love oneself is the beginning of a life-long romance.
OSCAR WILDE

I feel so good that I'm going to kiss myself.
JAMES BROWN

I don't like myself, I'm crazy about myself.
MAE WEST

We are all worms, but I believe I am a glowworm.
WINSTON CHURCHILL

Without self-love it is impossible to love others.
HERMANN HESSE

The most profound relationship we'll ever have
is the one with ourselves.

SHIRLEY MACLAINE

I continue to explain that no matter what their problem
seems to be, there is only one thing I ever work on with
anyone, and this is Loving the Self.
Love is the miracle cure.
Loving ourselves works miracles in our lives.
LOUISE L. HAY

Self-love is the only weight-loss aid
that really works in the long run.
JENNY CRAIG

He who is in love with himself
has at least this advantage—
he won't encounter many rivals.
GEORG CHRISTOPH LICHTENBERG

Love yourself first and everything else falls into line.
You really have to love yourself to get anything done
in this world.
LUCILLE BALL

I'd date me!
BRAD PITT

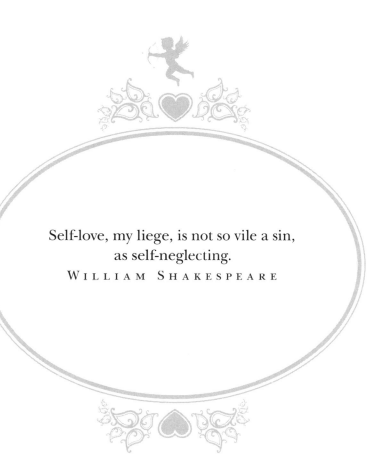

Self-love, my liege, is not so vile a sin,
as self-neglecting.

WILLIAM SHAKESPEARE

If you aren't good at loving yourself, you will have a
difficult time loving anyone, since you'll resent the time
and energy you give another person that you aren't even
giving to yourself.

BARBARA DE ANGELIS

Giving love to others is directly related to how much love
you have for yourself.

WAYNE DYER

Self-love is not opposed to the love of other people. You
cannot really love yourself and do yourself a favor
without doing people a favor, and vice versa.

KARL MENNINGER

A dog is the only thing on earth that loves you more
than you love yourself.

JOSH BILLINGS

Know yourself. Don't accept your dog's admiration as
conclusive evidence that you are wonderful.

ANN LANDERS

When you look back on your life
and try to figure out where you've been and
where you are going, when you look at your work,
your love affairs, your marriages, your children,
your pain, your happiness—
when you examine all that closely,
what you really find out is that the only person
you really go to bed with is yourself.
SHIRLEY MACLAINE

Seek not outside yourself, heaven is within.
MARY LOU COOK

You can explore the universe looking
for somebody who is more deserving of your love
and affection than you are yourself,
and you will not find that person anywhere.
BUDDHIST SAYING

Love is based first of all on developing
the love of one's life within.
Rather than looking for Mr. or Ms. Right out there,
It's *becoming* Mr. or Ms. Right.
HAROLD BLOOMFIELD

The ability to love oneself, combined with the ability
to love life, fully accepting that it won't last forever,
enables one to improve the quality of life.

BERNIE SIEGEL

A loving person lives in a loving world.
A hostile person lives in a hostile world:
Everyone you meet is your mirror.

KEN KEYES, JR.

My true relationship is my relationship with myself—all
others are simply mirrors of it. As I learn to love myself,
I automatically receive the love and appreciation from
others that I desire.

SHAKTI GAWAIN

Don't forget to love yourself.

SØREN KIERKEGAARD

End your day by privately looking directly into your eyes
in the mirror and saying,
"I love you!" Do this for thirty days
and watch how you transform.

MARK VICTOR HANSEN

Embraceable You

Hugs and Kisses

In the coldest February,
as in every month in every other year,
the best thing we can hold onto is each other.

LINDA ELLERBEE

They invented hugs to let people know you love them
without saying anything.

BIL KEANE

A silent hug means a thousand words
to the unhappy heart.

ANONYMOUS

Sometimes it's better to put love into hugs than to put it
into words.

ANONYMOUS

Nine times out of ten, when you extend your arms to
someone, they will step in, because basically they need
precisely what you need.

LEO BUSCAGLIA

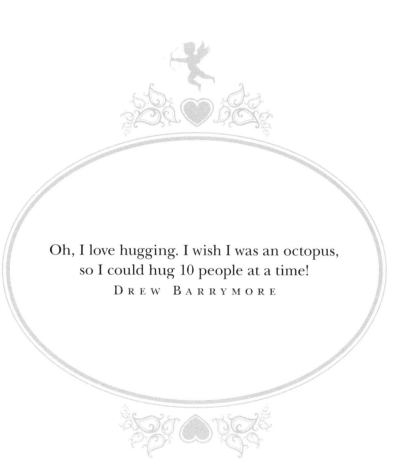

Oh, I love hugging. I wish I was an octopus,
so I could hug 10 people at a time!

DREW BARRYMORE

Millions and millions of years would still not give me half enough time to describe that tiny instant of all eternity when you put your arms around me and I put my arms around you.

JACQUES PRÉVERT

You can't wrap love in a box,
but you can wrap a person in a hug.

ANONYMOUS

A hug is like a boomerang—you get it back right away.

BIL KEANE

A hug is a smile with arms, a laugh with a stronger grip.

TERRI GUILLEMETS

No matter how hard you hug your money,
it never hugs back.

H. JACKSON BROWN, JR.

Everyone wants a hug and kiss.
It translates into any language.

GEORGETTE MOSBACHER

A career is a wonderful thing,
but you can't snuggle up to it on a cold night.

MARILYN MONROE

Offer hugs, not drugs.

ADINA LEBOWITZ

Arm ourselves for war? No!
All the arms we need are for hugging.

ANONYMOUS

A hug is a handshake from the heart.

ANONYMOUS

An emotional hug can be a thinking-of-you letter,
a thank-you card, or a phone call.

DAVID DENOTARIS

If you're angry at a loved one, hug that person. And mean
it. You may not want to hug—which is all the more reason
to do so. It's hard to stay angry when someone shows
they love you, and that's precisely what happens when we
hug each other.

WALTER ANDERSON

Hugging has no unpleasant side effects and is all natural.
There are no batteries to replace, it's inflation-proof
and non-fattening with no monthly payments. It's non-
taxable, non-polluting, and is,
of course, fully refundable.

A N O N Y M O U S

Hug Department. Always Open.

A N O N Y M O U S

Kiss, n.
A word invented by the poets as a rhyme for "bliss".

A M B R O S E   B I E R C E

A kiss is a lovely trick designed by nature to stop speech
when words become superfluous.

I N G R I D   B E R G M A N

The most eloquent silence;
that of two mouths meeting in a kiss.

A N O N Y M O U S

There is the kiss of welcome and of parting; the long,
lingering, loving, present one; the stolen, or the mutual
one; the kiss of love, of joy, and of sorrow; the seal of
promise and receipt of fulfillment.
THOMAS C. HALIBURTON

Kiss: A thing of no use to one, but prized by two.
ROBERT ZWICKEY

Kissing is a pleasant reminder
that two heads are better than one.
REX PROUTY

A kiss is strange. It's a living thing, a communication,
a whole wild emotion expressed in a simple moist touch.
MICKEY SPILLANE

A kiss can be a comma, a question mark,
or an exclamation point.
That's basic spelling that every woman ought to know.
MISTINGUETT

A kiss is like singing into someone's mouth.

DIANE ACKERMAN

A kiss is something you cannot give without taking
and cannot take without giving.

ANONYMOUS

'Tis a secret
Told to the mouth instead of to the ear.

EDMOND ROSTAND

Kisses are the messengers of love.

DANISH PROVERB

A kiss is a rosy dot over the "I" of loving.

CYRANO DE BERGERAC

Kisses are like grains of gold or silver found upon the
ground, of no value themselves, but precious as showing
that a mine is near.

GEORGE VILLIERS

Kissing is a means of getting two people so close together
that they can't see anything wrong with each other.

GENE YASENAK

Any man who can drive safely
while kissing a pretty girl
is simply not giving the kiss
the attention it deserves.
ALBERT EINSTEIN

Kissing is our greatest invention.
TOM ROBBINS

People who throw kisses are hopelessly lazy.
BOB HOPE

The doctor must have put (my pacemaker) in wrong.
Every time my husband kisses me,
the garage door goes up.
MINNIE PEARL

We did one of those quick,
awkward kisses where each of you
gets a nose in the eye.
CLIVE JAMES

I don't know how to kiss, or I would kiss you.
Where do the noses go?
INGRID BERGMAN IN
FOR WHOM THE BELL TOLLS

A kiss without a mustache is like an egg without salt.
SPANISH PROVERB

Q: Does your wife mind kissing you with that beard?
A: Not at all. She's happy to go through a forest
to get to a picnic.
ARCHIE MOORE

I wasn't kissing her. I was whispering in her mouth.
CHICO MARX

...let us kiss each other's eyes,
And laugh our love away.
WILLIAM BUTLER YEATS

I'd like to kiss you, but I just washed my hair.
BETTE DAVIS IN
THE CABIN IN THE COTTON

Kisses may not spread germs,
but they certainly lower resistance.
LOUISE ERICKSON

I have found men who didn't know how to kiss.
I've always found time to teach them.

M A E W E S T

A kiss without a hug is like a flower without the fragrance.
PROVERB

Anyone who's a great kisser I'm always interested in.
CHER

I kissed my first girl and smoked my first cigarette on the
same day. I haven't had time for tobacco since.
ARTURO TOSCANINI

Four sweet lips,
two pure souls, and one undying affection—
these are love's pretty ingredients for a kiss.
CHRISTIAN NESTELL BOVEE

In love there is always one who kisses,
and the other who offers the cheek.
FRENCH PROVERB

What I like about France is the kissing—
one of civilization's finest achievements.
ISABEL HUGGAN

May we kiss whom we please
And please whom we kiss.
ANONYMOUS

Kiss till the cow comes home.
FRANCIS BEAUMONT

Drink to me only with thine eyes,
And I will pledge with mine;
Or leave a kiss within the cup,
And I'll not look for wine.
BEN JONSON

Give me a thousand kisses and yet more;
And then repeat those that have gone before.
ANONYMOUS

One kiss more, and so farewell.
ANONYMOUS

Kissing power is stronger than will power.
ABIGAIL VAN BUREN

….then I did the simplest thing in the world. I leaned
down…and kissed him. And the world cracked open.

AGNES DE MILLE

…we kiss, and it feels like
we have just shrugged off the world.

JIM SHAHIN

With a kiss let us set out for an unknown world.

ALFRED DE MUSSET

My child, if you finally decide to let a man kiss you,
put your whole heart and soul into it.
No man likes to kiss a rock.

LADY CHESTERFIELD

I believe in long, slow, deep, soft,
wet kisses that last for three days.

KEVIN COSTNER IN *BULL DURHAM*

A kiss must last long to be enjoyed.

GREEK PROVERB

The kiss you take is better than you give.
WILLIAM SHAKESPEARE

Stolen kisses are always sweetest.
LEIGH HUNT

A legal kiss is never as good as a stolen one.
GUY DE MAUPASSANT

Stealing a kiss may be petty larceny,
but sometimes it's also grand.
ANONYMOUS

Be plain in dress, and sober in your diet;
In short, my deary, kiss me, and be quiet.
MARY WORTLEY MONTAGU

For it was not into my ear you whispered,
but into my heart. It was not my lips you kissed,
but my soul.
JUDY GARLAND

Soul meet soul on lovers' lips.
PERCY BYSSHE SHELLEY

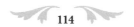

He kisses me and now I am someone else; someone else
in the pulse that repeats the pulse of my own veins and in
the breath that mingles with my breath.
GABRIELA MISTRAL

….how she felt when first he kissed her—
like a tub of roses
swimming in honey, cologne, nutmeg, and blackberries.
SAMUEL SULLIVAN COX

When she kissed him,
he melted like a lump of milk chocolate.
MARGE PIERCY

We turned on one another deep, drowned gazes, and
exchanged a kiss that reduced my bones to rubber
and my brain to gruel.
PETER DE VRIES

The sound of a kiss is not so loud as that of a cannon,
but its echo lasts a great deal longer.
OLIVER WENDELL HOLMES

Love Potion Number Nine

Love Conquers All

One word frees us of all the weight and pain of life:
That word is love.
SOPHOCLES

Love comforteth like sunshine after rain.
WILLIAM SHAKESPEARE

Love cures people—both the ones who give it
and the ones who receive it.
KARL MENNINGER

Our ability to pray for people
and surround them with love
makes an enormous difference
in how they feel and heal.
PEGGY HUDDLESTON

This is the miracle that happens every time to those who
really love: The more they give, the more they possess
of that precious nourishing love from which flowers and
children have their strength and which could help all
human beings if they would take it without doubting.
RAINER MARIA RILKE

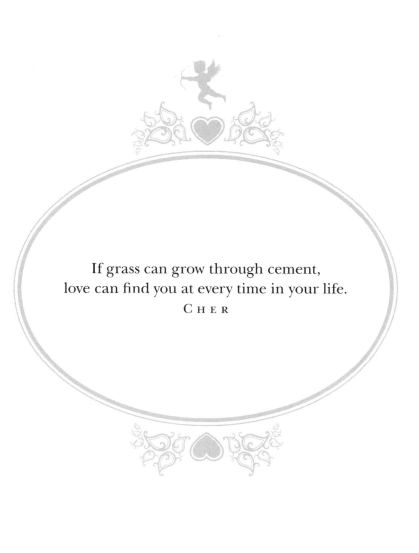

If grass can grow through cement,
love can find you at every time in your life.

Cher

We can look for every opportunity
to give and receive love,
to appreciate nature, to heal our wounds
and the wounds of others,
to forgive, and to serve.

JOAN BORYSENKO

One cannot be strong without love.
For love is not an irrelevant emotion;
it is the blood of life,
the power of reunion with the separated.

PAUL TILLICH

Love is a force more formidable than any other.
It is invisible—
it cannot be seen or measured,
yet it is powerful enough
to transform you in a moment,
and offer you more joy
than any material possession could.

BARBARA DE ANGELIS

There is no difficulty that enough love will not conquer,
no disease that enough love will not heal, no door that
enough love will not bridge, no wall that enough love
will not throw down, no sin that enough love will not
redeem… It makes no difference how deeply seated may
be the trouble, how hopeless the outlook, how muddled
the tangle, how great the mistake. A sufficient realization
of love will dissolve it all. If only you could love enough,
you could be the happiest and most powerful being in
the world…

EMMET FOX

Love, and love alone,
is capable of giving thee a happier life.

LUDWIG VAN BEETHOVEN

The cure for all ills and wrongs, the cares, the sorrows
and the crimes of humanity, all lie in the one word "love."
It is the divine that everywhere produces and restores life.

LYDIA MARIA CHILD

Love and food are equally vital to our sanity and survival.

KUO TZU

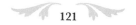

Love is the key to the solution
of the problems of the world.
MARTIN LUTHER KING, JR.

Love is the only sane and satisfactory answer
to the problems of human existence.
ERICH FROMM

Love alone is capable of uniting living beings in such a
way as to complete and fulfill them,
for it alone takes them and joins them
by what is deepest in themselves.
PIERRE TEILHARD DE CHARDIN

Then I grasped the meaning of the greatest secret
that human poetry and human thought
and belief have to impart:
The salvation of man is through love and in love.
VIKTOR FRANKL

If you have love in your life it can make up
for a great many things that are missing.
If you don't have love in your life,
no matter what else there is, it's not enough.
ANN LANDERS

Under the sustaining influence of love,
the physical body is always at its best.
It is probably true that more people are sick
from lack of love in their lives than
from all other causes put together.

ERIC BUTTERWORTH

Age does not protect you from love.
But love, to some extent, protects you from age.

JEANNE MOREAU

Where there is love there is life.

MAHATMA GANDHI

Treasure the love you receive above all.
It will survive long after your gold
and good health have vanished.

OG MANDINO

Kiss the place to make it well.

ANN TAYLOR

Where love reigns the impossible may be attained.
INDIAN PROVERB

It is love, not faith, that removes mountains.
GEORGE SAND

When I despair,
I remember that all through history the way
of truth and love has always won.
There have been tyrants
and murderers and for a time they seem invincible
but in the end, they always fall—
Think of it, ALWAYS.
MAHATMA GANDHI

Love accomplishes all things.
FRANCESCO PETRARCH

Darkness cannot drive out darkness;
only light can do that.
Hate cannot drive out hate;
only love can do that.
MARTIN LUTHER KING, JR.

There is a single magic, a single power, a single salvation,
and a single happiness, and that is called loving.

HERMANN HESSE

Love is one of the most powerful energies of the universe.
It is thousands of times stronger than anger,
resentment or fear.

SANAYA ROMAN

Love builds bridges where there are none.

R. H. DELANEY

Love creates an "us" without destroying the "me."

LEO BUSCAGLIA

To love deeply in one direction
makes us more loving in all others.

ANNE-SOPHIE SWETCHINE

Love's greatest gift is its ability to make everything it
touches sacred.

BARBARA DE ANGELIS

We do not judge the people we love.

JEAN-PAUL SARTRE

Love and you will be loved, and you will be able to do
all that you could not do unloved.

M A R Q U É S   D E   S A N T I L L A N A

Love is the only force capable of transforming
an enemy into a friend.

M A R T I N   L U T H E R   K I N G ,   J R .

Where there is great love, there are always miracles.

W I L L A   C A T H E R

When the power of love becomes more important than
the love of power, then will there be peace.

J I M I   H E N D R I X

All You Need Is Love

Unconditional Love

Love is all we have,
the only way that each can help the other.

E U R I P I D E S

Never waste an opportunity
to tell someone you love them.

H . J A C K S O N   B R O W N , J R .

If you judge people, you have no time to love them.

M O T H E R   T E R E S A

Don't look for love; give love—
and you will find love looking for you.

B E T H   B L A C K

Teach only love for that is what you are.

A   C O U R S E   I N   M I R A C L E S

Close the door when you get home from work, and
hug and kiss with someone special for at least fifteen
minutes—longer is better.

A N I T A   B A K E R

Do not seek perfection in a changing world.
Instead, perfect your love.

BUDDHA

Never succumb to the temptation of becoming bitter. As
you press for justice, be sure to move with dignity and
discipline, using only the weapon of Love.
MARTIN LUTHER KING, JR.

We can forgive as long as we love.
FRANÇOIS DUC DE LA ROCHEFOUCAULD

What the world really needs
is more love and less paperwork.
PEARL BAILEY

Do all things with love.
OG MANDINO

True love is unconquerable and irresistible. It goes on
gathering power and spreading itself, until eventually it
transforms everyone whom it touches.

MEHER BABA

True love is that which ennobles the personality, fortifies
the heart, and sanctifies the existence.

HENRI FRÉDÉRIC AMIEL

When souls really touch, it is forever. Then space and
time disappear, and all that remains is the consciousness
that we are not alone in life.

JOAN CHITTISTER

When we are motivated by goals that have deep meaning,
by dreams that need completion,
by pure love that needs expressing,
then we truly live life.

GREG ANDERSON

Perfect love is rare indeed—for to be a lover will require
that you continually have the subtlety of the very wise,
the flexibility of the child, the sensitivity of the artist, the
understanding of the philosopher, the acceptance of the
saint, the tolerance of the scholar and the fortitude of
the certain.

LEO BUSCAGLIA

Perfect love sometimes does not come
till the first grandchild.

WELSH PROVERB

When we find someone whose weirdness is compatible
with ours, we join up with them and fall into mutually
satisfying weirdness—
and call it love—true love.

ROBERT FULGHUM

We don't believe in rheumatism and true love
until after the first attack.

MARIE VON EBNER-ESCHENBACH

True love begins when nothing is looked for in return.

ANTOINE DE SAINT-EXUPÉRY

135

True love comes quietly,
without banners or flashing lights.
If you hear bells, get your ears checked.
ERICH SEGAL

If only one could tell true love from false love as one can
tell mushrooms from toadstools.
KATHERINE MANSFIELD

Our basic nature is incredible wisdom and unconditional
love. All we have to do is peel away the layers of beliefs
and conditioning collectively called the ego,
which prevent the light of our own true nature from
shining forth.
JOAN BORYSENKO

There isn't anyone you couldn't love
once you've heard their story.
MARY LOU KOWNACKI

Discovering an ability to love uncritically and totally has
been exhilarating. It's the sort of love that calls upon my
whole being, bringing all of my potential to life.

RONNIE FRIEDLAND

When we learn to love and serve everyone uncondition-
ally, we begin to experience that life is a cornucopia
which gives us far more security, sensations and power
than we really need to be happy.

KEN KEYES, JR. AND BRUCE BURKAN

Love and concern for all are not things some of us are
born with and others are not, Rather, they are results of
what we do with our minds: We can choose to transform
our minds so that they embody love, or we can allow
them to develop habits and false concepts of separation.

SHARON SALZBERG

Love everybody
and don't let flags and religions get in the way
of looking somebody in the eye and seeing the beauty
of the human person.

MAIREAD CORRIGAN MAGUIRE

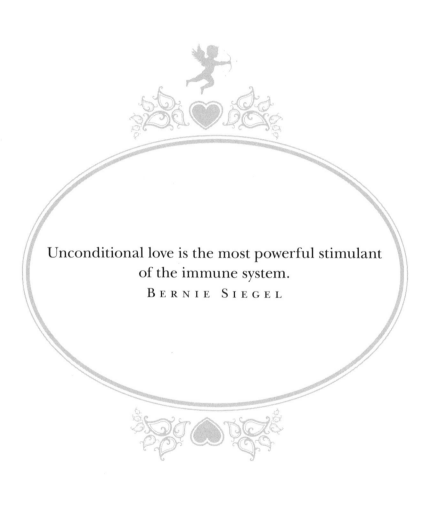

Unconditional love is the most powerful stimulant
of the immune system.

BERNIE SIEGEL

Unconditional love is loving your kids for who they are, not for what they do... I don't mean that we like or accept inappropriate behavior, but with unconditional love we love the children even at those times when we dislike their behavior. Unconditional love isn't something you will achieve every minute of every day. But it is the thought we must hold in our hearts every day.

STEPHANIE MARSTON

The ultimate lesson all of us have to learn is unconditional love, which includes not only others but ourselves as well.

ELISABETH KÜBLER-ROSS

Love is a state of being in which one is aware of the unity of all life.

RICHARD CHAMBERLAIN

I think I have discovered the highest good. It is love. This principle stands at the center of the cosmos.

MARTIN LUTHER KING, JR.

The final word is love.

DOROTHY DAY

INDEX TO AUTHORS

1 Corinthians 13:4-7 2
Ackerman, Diane. 12, 105
Adler, Mortimer J. 56
African proverb 80
Aldrich, Bess Streeter 16
Aleichem, Sholem 5
Alfred, Lord Tennyson 15, 59
Allen, Tim 28
Allen, Woody 13, 30
Amiel, Henri Frédéric 134
Anderson, Dale 74
Anderson, Greg 134
Anderson, John Louis 69
Anderson, Margaret 48
Anderson, Walter. 102
Angelou, Maya 52
Anonymous . . . . xxv, 6,
    31, 46, 52, 56, 75, 76, 90, 98, 100,
    102, 103, 106, 112, 114
Anouilh, Jean. 10
Arab proverb 51
Arndt, Bettina 70
Ashley, Elizabeth 46
Auden, W. H. 60
Aurelius, Marcus 52

Baba, Meher 134
Bacher, June Masters 16
Bailey, James Montgomery 36
Bailey, Pearl 132
Baker, Anita 130
Ball, Lucille 92
Balzac, Honoré de 16, 57, 82
Barrymore, Drew 99
Barth, Joseph 66
Battista, Orlando A. 46
Baudelaire, Charles 8
Bayly, Thomas Haynes. 51
Beaumont, Francis. 112
Beecher, Henry Ward 37, 80
Beethoven, Ludwig van 121
Benny, Jack. 74
Bergman, Ingrid 103, 108
Bierce, Ambrose. 103
Billings, Josh 8, 94
Black, Beth 130
Blanton, Smiley 5
Bloom, Amy 62
Bloomfield, Harold 95
Bombeck, Erma 67, 70, 73
Book of Common Prayer, The 62

Borysenko, Joan 120, 136
Bossuet, Jacques-Bénigne 48
Boteach, Rabbi Shmuley 75
Bovee, Christian Nestell 111
Bret, Antoine 36
Brothers, Joyce 20, 64, 76
Brown, Helen Gurley 26
Brown, James 90
Brown, Jr., H. Jackson . .71, 72, 100, 130
Browning, Elizabeth Barrett. . . 40
Buck, Pearl S. 88
Buddha. 131
Buddhist saying 95
Bulwer-Lytton, Edward 50
Burkan, Bruce 137
Buscaglia, Leo . . . 8, 22, 24, 31, 98, 126, 135
Bush, Barbara 84
Butterworth, Eric. 124
Campbell, Thomas 36
Camus, Albert 22
Cather, Willa 128
Catullus 56
Chagall, Marc. 14
Chamberlain, Richard 139
Cheever, Susan. 81
Cher 111, 119
Child, Lydia Maria. 121
Chittister, Joan. 134
Chödrön, Pema 53
Christie, Agatha. 44, 68, 80
Christie, May 16

Churchill, Winston 90
Clark, Frank A. 85
Clarke, Jean Illsley. 41
Coelho, Paulo. 25
Coleridge, Samuel Taylor 50
Connolly, Billy 65
Cook, Mary Lou. 95
Cooney, Joan Ganz 86
Cosby, Bill. 75
Cossman, E. Joseph. 16
Costner, Kevin 113
Course in Miracles, A 23, 130
Courtenay, Bryce 4
Cox, Samuel Sullivan 115
Craig, Jenny 92
Crawford, Joan. 10
Croft, Roy. 41
Crosby, Norm. 37
Dahl, Arlene. 78
Danish proverb 106
Davis, Bette 109
Davis, George. 27
Davis, Miles 55
Day, Dorothy 140
De Angelis, Barbara . . 71, 94, 120, 126
de Bergerac, Cyrano 106
de Mille, Agnes 113
De Vries, Peter 115
Delaney, R. H. 126
DeNotaris, David 102
Dickens, Charles 52
Dietrich, Marlene 30

Disraeli, Benjamin 35, 72
Dostoevsky, Fyodor 46
Drabble, Margaret 86
Dressler, Marie 20
Drummond, Henry 23
Duke, Patty 45
Dussault, Ed 80
Dyer, Wayne 7, 94
Edgeworth, Maria 50
Einstein, Albert 27, 34, 107
Ellerbee, Linda 98
Emerson, Ralph Waldo . 20, 52, 54
Emory, Stewart 7, 31
Erhard, Werner 23
Erickson, Louise 109
Erskine, John 5
Étienne, Henri 34
Euripides 130
Fechtner, Leopold 48
Fiterman, Linda 73
Fitzgerald, Zelda 53
Fleming, Anne Taylor 76
Fox, Emmet 121
Franken, Rose 59
Frankl, Viktor 123
French proverb 12, 60, 111
Friedland, Ronnie 137
Fromm, Erich 43, 85, 123
Frost, Robert 8
Fulghum, Robert 135
Fuller, Thomas 22
Gabor, Eva 6
Gabor, Zsa Zsa 67, 69

Galeano, Eduardo 36
Galsworthy, John 17
Gandhi, Mahatma 124, 125
Garland, Judy 114
Garner, Cindy 69, 70
Garner, James 64
Garretty, Marion C 86
Gawain, Shakti 96
Goethe, Johann Wolfgang von . .13, 30
Goldsmith, Oliver 70
Goodman, Ellen 45
Gordon, Julius 8
Greek proverb 37, 113
Greer, Germaine 28
Griffith, Melanie 57
Guillemets, Terri 100
Hale, Clara 88
Haliburton, Thomas C 104
Halm, Friedrich 55
Hanh, Thich Nhat 3
Hansberry, Lorraine 30
Hansen, Mark Victor 96
Harris, Sydney J. 72
Havergal, Frances R 12
Hay, Louise L. 92
Hendrix, Jimi 128
Herbert, George 53
Herold, Don 63
Hesse, Hermann 42, 90, 126
Hill, Napoleon 59
Holmes, Oliver Wendell 2, 115
Hope, Bob 108

Houldsworth, Joe........... 88
Houssaye, Arsène............23
Howe, Edgar Watson...... 64, 67
Hower, Barbara............ 48
Huddleston, Peggy..........118
Huggan, Isabel.............111
Hugo, Victor..............17, 25
Hunt, Leigh................114
Indian proverb.............125
Ingram, Kay................57
Irving, Washington............4
Italian proverb........12, 15, 30
James, Clive...............108
Jerome, Jerome K............37
Jones, Franklin P..............2
Jong, Erica................ 66
Jonson, Ben................112
Jordan, Tenneva............ 83
Jung, Carl..................31
Keane, Bil............. 98, 100
Keillor, Garrison............ 26
Keller, Helen 23, 51
Kempis, Thomas à..........5, 13
Kerr, Jean..................67
Keyes, Jr., Ken......... 6, 96, 137
Kierkegaard, Søren.......... 96
King, Jr., Martin Luther .. 54, 122, 125, 128, 132, 139
Kownacki, Mary Lou.........136
Krishnamurti, J..............52
Kübler-Ross, Elisabeth 139
Kurshan, Neil.............. 85
Kurtz, Irma................ 82

Lady Chesterfield...........113
Lafayette, Marquis de 41
Landers, Ann........... 94, 123
Lao-Tzu....................13
Leach, Penelope 86
Lebowitz, Adina............102
Lebowitz, Fran.......... 28, 56
Lee, Robert G...............74
LeGuin, Ursula 29
Levenson, Sam.............. 43
Lewis, Richard..............55
Lewis, Sinclair 16
Lichtenberg, Georg Christoph. 92
Lindbergh, Anne Morrow..... 22
Longfellow, Henry Wadsworth ..28, 43
Lord Byron................. 34
Loren, Sophia 82
Luther, Martin..............72
Mabie, Hamilton Wright...... 83
Macdonald, George.......... 50
MacLaine, Shirley 91, 95
Maguire, Mairead Corrigan...137
Mandino, Og 53, 124, 133
Mansfield, Katherine.........136
Marquis, Don............... 40
Marston, Stephanie...... 85, 139
Marx, Chico................109
Marx, Groucho 88
Maupassant, Guy de 114
Maurois, André 71, 76
McCord, Nancy 62
McIntosh, Joan.............. 88

McKuen, Rod 32, 46
McLaughlin, Mignon 25
Mencken, H. L. 28
Menninger, Karl 94, 118
Merton, Thomas 12
Miller, Henry 21
Mistinguett. 104
Mistral, Gabriela 115
Mitford, Nancy. 27
Mohnke, Kathy. 63
Monroe, Marilyn 101
Montagu, Mary Wortley 114
Montaigne, Michel de 64
Moore, Archie 109
Moore, Clement C. 36
Moreau, Jeanne 124
Morgan, Charles 26
Morley, Christopher xxiii
Mosbacher, Georgette. 100
Mother Teresa 17, 130
Murphy, Christy. 51
Murray, Joe. 77
Musset, Alfred de. 113
Necker, Suzanne 59
Newman, Nanette 72
Nicolson, Harold 78
Nietzsche, Friedrich 50
Nouwen, Henri J. M. 53
Ortega, Clara. 41
Ovid 27
Paddock, Benjamin Henry 80
Paltrow, Gwyneth. 20
Panin, Ivan. 51

Parker, Dorothy 9
Parnell, Thomas 54
Pascal, Blaise 4
Pearl, Minnie 108
Peck, M. Scott. 5, 7
Petrarch, Francesco. 125
Picasso, Pablo. 17
Piercy, Marge 115
Pitt, Brad 92
Polish proverb 80
Prentice, George
    Dennison 57
Prévert, Jacques 100
Proust, Marcel 51
Prouty, Rex. 104
Proverb 111
Ray, Rudolph 71
Renard, Jules 10
Repplier, Agnes 75
Reuben, David Robert. 64
Richter, Jean Paul 14
Rilke, Rainer Maria. 43, 118
Robbins, Tom. 108
Rochefoucauld, François, Duc
    de la. 31, 132
Rogers, Fred. 4, 43
Rogers, Rosemary 34
Rolland, Romain 57
Roman, Sanaya 17, 126
Rorem, Ned 10
Rostand, Edmond 40, 106
Rowland, Helen 18, 27, 62
Rudner, Rita. 67, 69

Ruskin, John. 86
Russell, Bertrand. 2
Russell, Earl 76
Russian proverb 38
Saint Augustine 15
Saint-Exupéry, Antoine de . . 13, 49, 135
Salzberg, Sharon 137
San Juan de la Cruz. 32
Sand, George 36, 125
Santillana, Marqués de 128
Sartre, Jean-Paul 127
Sayers, Dorothy L. 45
Schneider, Bob. 8
Schulz, Charles 16, 17, 46
Schumann, Robert 55
Schweitzer, Albert 14
Scott, Sir Walter. 2
Scott-Maxwell, Florida 83
Segal, Erich 136
Shain, Merle. 10
Shakespeare, William. . 93, 114, 118
Shahin, Jim. 113
Shaw, George Bernard 36
Shelley, Percy Bysshe 114
Shoales, Ian 11
Siegel, Bernie. 96, 138
Signoret, Simone 78
Slogan. 88
Smith, Alexander. 6
Smith, Sydney. 63
Socrates 69
Sophocles 118
Spanish proverb. 108
Spillane, Mickey. 104
Stephens, James 50
Stewart, Rod. 70
Stone, Elizabeth. 82
Stone, Irving 47
Sullivan, Harry Stack 6
Sunde, Karen 26
Swetchine, Anne-Sophie. 126
Tagore, Rabindranath. 11
Tasso, Torquato 28
Taylor, Ann. 124
Taylor, Jeremy. 10
Teilhard de Chardin, Pierre. . .123
Tempelsman, Cathy Rindner . . 83
Thoreau, Henry David 30
Thurber, James 7
Tillich, Paul 120
Tomlin, Lily 11
Toscanini, Arturo 111
Toynbee, Arnold 14
Twain, Mark 66, 73
Tzu, Kuo. 121
Updike, John 55
Upton, George. 41
Ustinov, Peter. 7
Van Buren, Abigail 112
Van Gogh, Vincent 15
Vega, Lope de 14, 15
Villiers, George 106
Viorst, Judith 11, 40
Viscott, David. 20
Voltaire. 15

von Ebner-Eschenbach, Marie . . 135
von Furstenberg, Diane 87
Welch, Raquel 83
Welsh proverb 135
West, Mae 22, 90, 110
Whitman, Walt 90
Wilde, Oscar 11, 25, 54, 58, 90
Williams, Paul 23
Williamson, Marianne 4, 22

Woodward, Joanne 74
Wordsworth, William 12
Yasenak, Gene 106
Yeats, William Butler 109
Yglesias, Helen 25
Yiddish proverb 18
Yogananda, Paramahansa 53
Youngman, Henny 75, 78
Zwickey, Robert 104

ABOUT THE AUTHOR

ALLEN KLEIN is an award-winning professional speaker and bestselling author who lives in San Francisco. He teaches people worldwide how to use humor to deal with not-so-funny stuff. In addition to this book, Klein is also the author of *The Healing Power of Humor, Change Your Life!: A Little Book of Big Ideas, Inspiration for a Lifetime,* and *The Art of Living Joyfully,* among others.

For more information about Klein or his presentations go to www.allenklein.com or e-mail him at humor@allenklein.com.

To Our Readers

Viva Editions publishes books that inform, enlighten, and entertain. We do our best to bring you, the reader, quality books that celebrate life, inspire the mind, revive the spirit, and enhance lives all around. Our authors are practical visionaries: people who offer deep wisdom in a hopeful and helpful manner. Viva was launched with an attitude of growth and we want to spread our joy and offer our support and advice where we can to help you live the Viva way: vivaciously!

We're grateful for all our readers and want to keep bringing you books for inspired living. We invite you to write to us with your comments and suggestions, and what you'd like to see more of. You can also sign up for our online newsletter to learn about new titles, author events, and special offers.

Viva Editions
2246 Sixth St.
Berkeley, CA 94710
www.vivaeditions.com
(800) 780-2279
Follow us on Twitter @vivaeditions
Friend/fan us on Facebook